Williamson W Publishing

GARDEN FUN!

Indoors & Out;
In Pots & Small Spots

Vicky Congdon

Illustrations by
Heather Barberie

D1313755

Quick Starts for Kids!™

WILLIAMSON PUBLISHING • CHARLOTTE, VERMONT

Library of Congress Cataloging-in-Publication Data

Congdon, Vicky, 1958–
    Garden fun! : indoors & out, in pots & small spots / Vicky Congdon ; illustrations by
Heather Barberie.
        p. cm. -- (Quicks starts for kids)
    Includes index.
    Summary: Provides step-by-step instructions for twenty-eight indoor or outdoor
gardening adventures, including a salad garden window box, a spiral flower garden, and
a butterfly paradise in a patio pot.
    ISBN 1-885593-69-4 (pbk.)
    1. Gardening--Juvenile literature. 2. Gardening--Study and teaching--Activity
programs--Juvenile literature. [1. Gardening.] I. Barberie, Heather, ill. II. Title. III.
Series.

SB457 .C645 2002
635--dc21

2002016820

Quick Starts for Kids!™ series editor: **Susan Williamson**

Interior design: **Dana Pierson**

Interior illustrations: **Heather Barberie, Rum Raisin Design**

Cover design: **Marie Ferrante-Doyle**

Cover illustrations: **Michael Kline**

Printing: **Capital City Press**

Williamson Publishing Co.
P.O. Box 185
Charlotte, VT 05445
(800) 234-8791

Manufactured in the United States of America

10 9 8 7 6 5 4 3 2

Dedication

To my mom, Mary Eleanor
Schenke, who passed on
her love of gardening to
her three daughters, and to
my dad, Bob Congdon,
who supports all my
endeavors with such
enthusiasm.

Acknowledgments

With thanks to Susan
Williamson, who helped
me squeeze my enthusiasm
for gardening into 64
pages and to share it with
all kids, whether they
garden on a windowsill,
in a big backyard, or
somewhere in between.

Contents

Let's Get Growing!

My very first plant was a begonia that my mom brought home for my windowsill. I would take frequent breaks from my homework to take care of it, keeping it very well watered and eagerly snipping off dead blossoms and leaves (Oops! Was that one still growing?) with a pair of nail scissors. All things considered, the plant held up quite well until I started actually digging in the dirt with the scissors to see if the roots had grown at all since I'd gotten it! While I wouldn't recommend caring for any plant quite this enthusiastically, that kind of curiosity about and fascination with green, growing things is what makes gardening fun!

Here's a collection of more than 28 activities to let you explore the fun of gardening, indoors and out. Did you know you don't need a yard to grow strawberries or several weeks' worth of fresh salad veggies? Would you like to watch a bug-eating bog plant catch itself a snack right on your windowsill or to try your hand at pollinating corn or pumpkin plants (it's not hard!)? You can have garden "pets," too: compost-making worms (that rely on you for care and feeding), gorgeous butterflies that visit your yard or deck because you planted their favorite flowers, and feathered friends that raise their family in the birdhouse you "grew" just for them.

Whether you choose something quick and easy or go for a project that will keep you in the garden all season long, the handy symbols that appear with each activity will tell you at a glance what's required for success.

indoor   outdoor   sun   shade   container   outdoor spot

Even if you've never planted a seed before, you'll find all the how-to gardening information you need in the *Quick Starts*™ Growing Guide (pages 56–60). Don't be surprised if your new skills blossom into a lifetime love of green-thumb adventures!

So dig in! Remember, with gardening, the *more* dirt under your fingernails, the *better!*

Quick Starts™ Green-Thumb Adventures

Can't wait to dig in? Well, you've turned to the right page! These gardening adventures take only a couple of hours at most. Plus, you'll find both indoor and outdoor adventures for four seasons of fun.

Fast-Food Windowsill Salad Garden

 or

A bright, sunny windowsill (indoors or out) or a small container in the yard will provide you with fresh pickings for a delicious salad that you grew yourself! Tuck in some seeds of an edible flower like nasturtiums to make the planting — and the salad — even more colorful. If you have space for two planters, start the second one two weeks after the first for a steady supply of salad fixings. If your indoor plants need more sun, try a grow light (a special plant light available at hardware stores or garden centers).

What you need

Window box or other container with drainage holes

Planting mix*

Seeds or plants: See MINI-MUNCHES, at right, plus nasturtiums (optional)

Trowel

Hose or watering can

Sunny window or outdoor spot

Sharp knife (optional; for use with grown-up help)

Scissors

Fertilizer*

Mini-Munches

These veggie varieties are perfect for your miniature salad garden. See RESOURCES, page 61, if you can't find them at a garden center.

Beets: Little Ball

Carrots: Little Finger, Thumbelina

Lettuce: Little Gem, Tom Thumb

Radishes: Easter Egg (red, purple, and white)

Scallions: Evergreen Long White Bunching

Spinach: Space

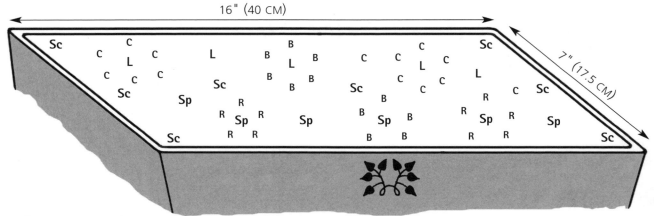

What you do

To grow your salads

1. Fill the container about three-fourths full of the planting mix. Plant* the seeds. Water* well.

This arrangement will provide you with plenty to nibble on. Plant two seeds at each spot; thin* one out if they both sprout. Plant the nasturtiums (if using) along the edges, and let them trail over the sides.

B = beets	**L** = lettuce	**Sc** = scallions
C = carrots	**R** = radishes	**Sp** = spinach

2. Place the container in full sun.
   Keep the soil moist but not soaking wet. Once the seedlings are up, thin* as necessary.

See Quick Starts™ Growing Guide, pages 56–60.

To harvest your salads

3. For about a month's supply of salad greens, as the plants grow, snip off the outer lettuce and spinach leaves and some of the fresh, green beet tops (but don't take too many, or the beet underground won't develop).

When the lettuce and spinach plants get bigger, you can either pull out the entire plants, or use the sharp knife to cut it off just above the soil — it will regrow! (This trick works only once, though.)

As soon as the radishes, scallions, beets, and carrots are big enough to eat, start harvesting — small and tender means maximum flavor. Try grating the raw beets on top of your salad to add a colorful (and healthy!) crunch.

4. Fertilize regularly to keep your window box delivering the produce!

Seeds or plants?

These vegetable plants are happiest when you plant them from seeds in their permanent spots. This is especially true for the carrots, beets, and radishes — after the seeds sprout, they immediately start to form a long, skinny root called a taproot, *and they* really *don't like to be disturbed while they're working on that.*

But if you're in a hurry for homegrown salad, look for transplants *("baby" plants) at the garden center. Be extra-gentle when you plant* them, keeping as much of the soil around the roots as possible. Give tiny lettuce plants a day or so to settle in before you put the container in bright sun, or they may wilt.*

Circle-of-Bloom Bouquet Garden

  or

or

All it takes is a trip to the garden center to pick out flowers in your favorite colors, and you're ready to brighten a corner of the yard, patio, or stoop with rings of color. As a bonus, you'll have flowers for picking all season long.

What you need

Flour

Patch of soil* prepared for planting or a large planter filled with planting mix*

Plants: colorful annuals*, one type for each ring

Trowel

Hose or watering can

Fertilizer*

See Quick Starts™ Growing Guide, pages 56–60.

Choosing your flowers

Decide how big you want your planting area to be and mark it out *before* you go plant shopping. That way, you'll know how many plants you'll need for each circle. Annuals* usually come in little packs of four or six — plan on one plant for every 6" (15 cm).

Here are some easy-to-grow flowers (and their typical colors) to look for at the garden center.

✿ **We want sun!** ageratum (blue); celosia (red, yellow); marigolds, especially Tangerine Gem and Lemon Gem (orange, yellow); nasturtiums (red, orange, yellow); nicotiana (red, pink, white, lime green); petunias (blue, red, pink, purple, white), zinnias (yellow, red, orange, pink)

✿ **I'm made for the shade!** impatiens (comes in all shades of red, pink, orange, plus white, and thrives in little or no sun)

What you do

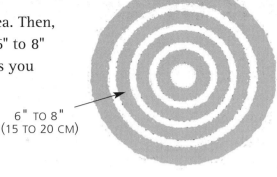

1. Use the flour to mark the center of the planting area. Then, sprinkle the flour to form a series of circles about 6" to 8" (15 to 20 cm) apart. You can have as many rings as you like, depending on how much space you have.

6" TO 8"
(15 TO 20 CM)

2. Remove the plants from their containers (see PLANTING PLANTS, page 58) and arrange them along the flour lines, zigzagging them slightly. Start with the tallest types in the center and work your way out to the shortest (check the little tags that come with the plants for the full-grown heights). Try different arrangements until you like the way it all looks.

3. Now, plant* the flowers. Water* thoroughly after planting. Looks great, doesn't it?

4. Water and fertilize throughout the growing season.

Quick Starts Tips!™

Off with their heads!

To keep your flower garden looking its best and covered with blooms, snip off the flower blossoms once they die (this is called *deadheading*). The plants will not only look prettier, they'll also keep putting out new flowers.

My Green-Thumb Journal

What better way to show off your gardening adventures than with a unique garden scrapbook? You can store seed packets or display cool-looking seeds (clear plastic photo sleeves and small zip-locking plastic bags are handy holders), track plant growth, and keep weather records. It's also the perfect place to create garden-inspired artwork and display photos of one-of-a-kind gardens.

What you need

For the cover: 2 sheets of stiff paper, hole punch, and brass fasteners, yarn, or shoelaces

Cover decorations: Dried flowers and leaves, stickers, markers, illustrations from old garden catalogs and magazines, seeds, tempera paints and brushes

Glue

White paper for the journal pages

What you do

1. Decorate one sheet of stiff paper for the front cover. For fun, why not make nature prints? Paint one side of leaves, petals, flowers (on stems), or seedpods with one or more colors of tempera paint and press the painted side on the paper. Great for page border patterns, too!

PETALS

LEAVES

2. Place the white paper between the two covers, punch holes, and insert brass fasteners or tie together with the yarn.

3. Now you're ready to record your gardening fun!

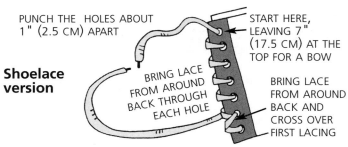

Shoelace version

PUNCH THE HOLES ABOUT 1" (2.5 CM) APART

BRING LACE FROM AROUND BACK THROUGH EACH HOLE

START HERE, LEAVING 7" (17.5 CM) AT THE TOP FOR A BOW

BRING LACE FROM AROUND BACK AND CROSS OVER FIRST LACING

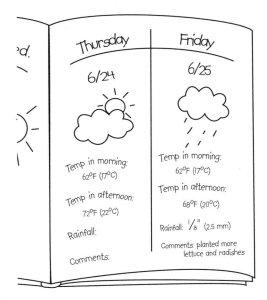

All good gardeners are weather-watchers!

Chart the growth of your plants. To grow a monster pumpkin, see pages 50 to 53.

❋ More Garden Fun!

Make a flower press *to dry the blossoms and leaves of your favorite flowers to decorate your journal. Spread them out on several sheets of paper towel and cover them with several more sheets. Stack a heavy book on top. Let them dry until they are crisp like paper (it may take a couple of weeks).*

To use, gently glue in place; let dry. Then lightly brush with a diluted glue mixture (1 part glue to 3 parts water).

Welcome Your Worms!

You'll beg to take out the garbage when you can feed it to your bin of red wiggler worms! These small, quiet creatures spend their days munching away on your kitchen scraps, making good, rich fertilizer for your garden. Now, how could your parents refuse to get you some (or maybe 1,000!) of these helpful, well-behaved pets?

What you need

Drill (for use with grown-up help)
Wooden or plastic bin (no more than 1½'/45 cm deep) with a lid
1" (2.5 cm) strips of old newspaper
Small amount of soil
Water
Red wiggler worms (see box, page 15)
Wooden blocks
Large sheet of plastic or several layers of old newspaper

Note: A 2' x 3' x 1' container (60 x 90 x 30 cm) is a great size for the kitchen waste from a family of four.

What you do

To prepare the worms' bed

1. With a grown-up's help, drill 10 or 12 holes in the bottom of the bin for drainage and airflow. (Don't worry; the worms won't escape!)

2. Fill the bin about three-fourths full of newspaper strips; add a handful of soil (to provide grit in the worm's gizzard so it can digest its food). Mix everything together and moisten it, letting the water soak in.

   The bedding has to be damp (a worm needs to keep its skin moist so it can breathe through it) but not too wet. Squeeze a handful of bedding — if you get more than a few drops of water, pour off the excess or let the box dry out a bit.

3. Place the worms in the box and watch them immediately start to burrow down where it's dark and damp! Then, put the lid on.

4. Place the box on wooden blocks (for air circulation) with plastic or newspapers underneath it where the air temperature will be between 55° and 77°F (13° to 25°C).

To feed the worms

A pound (500 g) of red wigglers (about 1,000 worms) will eat about three pounds (1.5 kg) of food a week. You can feed them fruit and vegetable scraps, coffee grounds, tea leaves, crushed eggshells (for calcium) — even those "science projects" from the back of the fridge are OK. Just avoid meat, dairy products, and oily foods. Add small amounts of food each day, placing them in different sections of the bin.

To remove the castings

Your worms are like tiny composting bins: The food scraps and bedding go in one end, and dark, crumbly *castings* (everything the worm doesn't digest) come out the other end. Using worms to make compost is called *vermicomposting*. The castings are actually poisonous to the worms, so it's important to remove them about once a month. Plus, it's fun! Really!

Spread out the contents of the bin on the plastic sheet. Remove the top layer of bedding and let the worms move down to escape the light. Separate out the dark, crumbly castings.

COCOONS

WORMS

CASTINGS

Keep removing the top layer and then waiting a minute or so, until you are left with a pile of worms. See if you spot any of the small round cocoons, which can contain up to 20 eggs (although usually only three or four worms hatch). The cocoons turn red when the worms are ready to wiggle out.

Put the worms, a few cocoons, and the bedding back in the bin and you're ready to roll! Add fresh bedding and a little more soil about every four months.

Give your garden plants or your houseplants a real treat by sprinkling some nutrient-packed castings on the soil around them. Now you're a great vermicomposter — or make that *wormi-*composter!

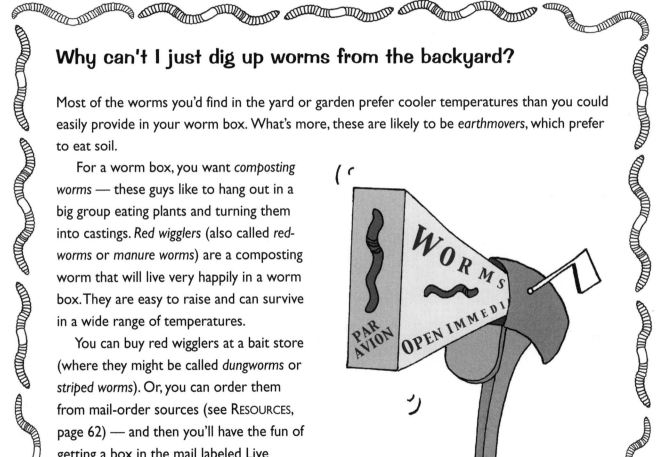

Why can't I just dig up worms from the backyard?

Most of the worms you'd find in the yard or garden prefer cooler temperatures than you could easily provide in your worm box. What's more, these are likely to be *earthmovers*, which prefer to eat soil.

For a worm box, you want *composting worms* — these guys like to hang out in a big group eating plants and turning them into castings. *Red wigglers* (also called *redworms* or *manure worms*) are a composting worm that will live very happily in a worm box. They are easy to raise and can survive in a wide range of temperatures.

You can buy red wigglers at a bait store (where they might be called *dungworms* or *striped worms*). Or, you can order them from mail-order sources (see RESOURCES, page 62) — and then you'll have the fun of getting a box in the mail labeled Live Worms! Open Immediately!

Make a Rain Gauge

 and

With this simple rain gauge, you can be sure your plants are getting enough water. A wide-mouth jar works best for collecting rainfall. Then, use a narrower jar to make the rain gauge, so you can precisely measure even very small amounts of rain.

Record the rainfall amounts in your journal (see MY GREEN-THUMB JOURNAL, pages 10 to 11). Most garden vegetables and flowers need about 1" to 1½" (2.5 to 3.5 cm) of water a week.

What you need

Ruler
Wide-mouth collecting jar
Water
Straight-sided clear jar about 1" to 1½" (2.5 to 3.5 cm) in diameter for the gauge
Permanent marker

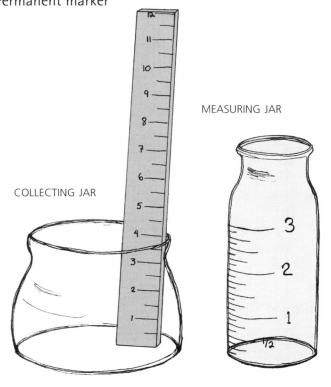

COLLECTING JAR

MEASURING JAR

What you do

1. Set the ruler in your collecting jar and fill it with 1" (2.5 cm) of water. Pour the water into the narrow jar. Label the level of the water as 1" (2.5 cm) and then divide that into smaller increments, such as ⅛", ¼", and ½" (2.5 mm, 5 mm, and 1 cm).

2. Set your collecting jar in an open area outdoors. Measure the amount of rain in your rain gauge every day (and then empty it) and record your measurements. (You may have to leave your jar out longer to have a measurable amount of precipitation, depending on the time of year and the seasonal rainfall patterns where you live.) Is it time to drag out the hose?

Pot Luck:
Sowing & Growing in Containers

"But I don't think I have space for a garden."
Hmmm ... let's think again. You've got a
windowsill, right? A deck or apartment
balcony? How about a set of sunny front
steps just begging for some green,
growing plants?

   Let's face it, *anyone* can be a
container gardener — indoors or out!
You see, you *can* be
a green-thumb extraordinaire,
with or without a backyard.

17

Indoor Magic

Butterfly Topiary

Perhaps you've seen an outdoor topiary — a bush or tree that's been clipped and formed into a shape, like a big green animal, for example. Well, you can have your very own windowsill topiary — a potted ivy will quickly grow into whatever shape you like! And all you need to do to keep your ivy creation healthy and happy is to give it bright light and regular watering.

What you need

Two 8" to 10" (20 to 25 cm) sections of wire
(10-gauge wire is easy to bend)
Pliers
2 pipe cleaners or wire-stemmed artificial
flowers
Thin wire (for wiring butterfly together)
5" to 6" (12.5 to 15 cm) section of wire coat
hanger or other stiff wire
Potted ivy plant

What you do

1. Bend the two sections of wire into wing shapes.

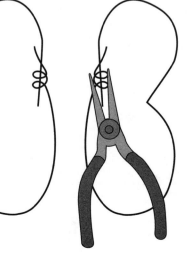

PRESS WIRE
ENDS FLAT
WITH PLIERS

2. Wire the butterfly together as shown.

3. Gently but securely push the end of the coat hanger into the soil near the plant. Train the stems of the ivy along the wings — they won't need much encouragement!

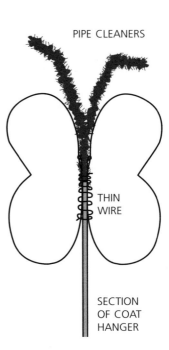

PIPE CLEANERS

THIN WIRE

SECTION OF COAT HANGER

A star and a heart are also easy wire shapes.

Shape up with more topiary tricks!

Brighten a tabletop or mantel with some holiday color (makes a great gift, too)!

Terrific Terrariums

Green up any corner of a room with a terrarium, a magical little garden under glass. Many terrarium plants will do fine where the light is low (can be on a table in the center of a room) or moderate (on a windowsill but out of direct sunlight). Some carnivorous plants will also be quite happy in your terrarium (see Bring on the Bug-Munchers, *pages 22 to 23); they require very bright sun and no lid.*

A large glass jar, a shallow glass dish, even an old fishbowl or aquarium all make perfect terrarium containers (just place a piece of plastic food wrap over the top if you don't have a lid).

What you need

Small gravel to cover bottom of jar
Large clean glass container with lid
Planting mix*
Sheet of paper (optional)
Activated charcoal (optional)
Spoon (you'll need a long-handled one if the
    container is deep or has a narrow opening)
Plants (see Plants for Terrariums, at right)
Watering can

Plants for terrariums

Here are some easy-to-grow plants that will be quite happy in your mini–rain forest.

bird's nest sansevieria   strawberry begonia
Fittonia   Swedish ivy
maidenhair fern   wintergreen (smells
Peperomia   like mint!)
spider plant

See Quick Starts™ Growing Guide, pages 56–60.

What you do

1. Place about ½" (1 cm) of gravel in the bottom of the container. Fill it with 5" or 6" (12.5 to 15 cm) of the planting mix. (Rolling the paper into a funnel makes it easy to fill a container with a narrow opening.) Mixing in a handful of activated charcoal will help keep everything fresh in that damp environment. That's all there is to it — now you're ready to plant!

2. For each plant: Dig a hole with the spoon. Gently remove the plant from its plastic pot (see PLANTING PLANTS, page 58) and settle it into the hole, maneuvering it into place with the other end of the spoon, if necessary. Push the soil back around the plant.

3. Water lightly and set the terrarium in a spot where it will get bright to moderate light, but not direct sunlight. Place the lid on the terrarium.

PLANTING MIX ⟶

GRAVEL ⟶

Quick Starts Tips!™

Terrarium care

- Most of the time, your terrarium will water itself! The water in the air inside the jar will *condense* (turn to droplets), and "rain" on the plants. What a perfect arrangement!

  But your terrarium plants are relying on you to keep an eye on things. Check regularly to be sure there's no more than a faint mist of condensation in the jar. If too much moisture builds up inside the jar or on the leaves of the plants, partially or completely remove the lid and let things dry out a bit. Water only when the terrarium looks really dry.

- Cut off dead leaves and remove them (so they don't rot in there). Pinch or cut back your plants if they get too big.

Bring on the Bug-Munchers!

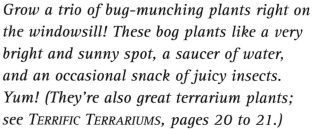

Grow a trio of bug-munching plants right on the windowsill! These bog plants like a very bright and sunny spot, a saucer of water, and an occasional snack of juicy insects. Yum! (They're also great terrarium plants; see Terrific Terrariums, *pages 20 to 21.)*

If you can't find these plants at a local greenhouse or florist, see Resources, *page 61, for mail-order sources.*

What you need

Potted plants: pitcher plant (*Sarracenia purpurea* or *Nepenthes ventricosa*), sundew, and Venus flytrap

For each plant: shallow saucer filled with distilled water (from supermarket or drugstore)

Windowsill in full sun

What you do

Keep it sunny and steamy

Set each potted plant in a saucer and place it on a windowsill. Refill the dish and water the plants (with distilled water) as necessary. Be careful not to overwater the soil. If your house is very dry, mist the plants with a spray bottle or set a large soda bottle (bottom cut off and cap and label removed) over each one.

Gather some bugs

You can feed your plants houseflies, moths, gnats, fruit flies, beetles, and other small bugs. A bug a week is a good guideline. For the Venus flytrap, look for insects no more than one-fourth the size of the trap. (Sqeamish about bugs? You don't have to feed them to your plants, and they'll do just fine.)

Give it a rest

If your plant is growing very slowly (and in the case of the flytrap, stops growing new traps), it may be going into *dormancy* (a seasonal rest period). Check with the nursery where you purchased your plant for more information.

How carnivorous plants eat

In the wild, these carnivorous *(meat-eating) plants grow in* bogs, *very wet environments where there is little or no soil. The plants need to look for additional sources of nutrients, so they attract bugs with sweet-smelling nectar. The plants don't actually eat the bug; they crush its body and digest the fluids. (So think about it before you try to feed your flytrap a bug that's been lying on the windowsill for several days — how much juice do you think is in that?)*

Pitcher plant: *The insects fall into the* pitcher *(the narrow tube or cup formed by the leaves) where they're digested. Gently peek into the tube — can you see the arms, legs, antennae, and other indigestible body parts? Cool, huh?*

Sundew: *Gnats, fruit flies, and other small bugs stick to the gluey substance that covers the plant and are slowly digested. (Look at how the drops covering the plant sparkle in the sun — can you see how this plant got its name?)*

Venus flytrap: *Without a doubt, this plant is the most exciting one to watch! When insects touch the little hairs inside the "mouth," it quickly closes, and the trap gradually squeezes all the "juice" out of the bug. Several days later, the trap opens and you can see the flattened remains. The traps are delicate, and they only open and shut about four or five times before they die.*

Outdoor Fun

Soccer Star's Garden

How about a victory garden to celebrate a winning season? Using your outgrown cleats and an old soccer ball for planters will surely make the wackiest one anyone has ever seen!

What you need

Old soccer ball
Bench vise
Drill with medium-sized drill
    bit (for grown-up use only)
X-Acto saw with heavy-duty
    blade or utility knife with
    heavy-duty blade (for
    grown-up use only)
Old cleats or sneakers
Planting mix*
Trowel
Flower seeds or plants
Hose or watering can
Fertilizer*

What you do

1. Secure the soccer ball in the vise.

See Quick Starts™ Growing Guide, pages 56–60.

Once you've secured the ball in the vise, please ask a grown-up to do the drilling and cutting for you.

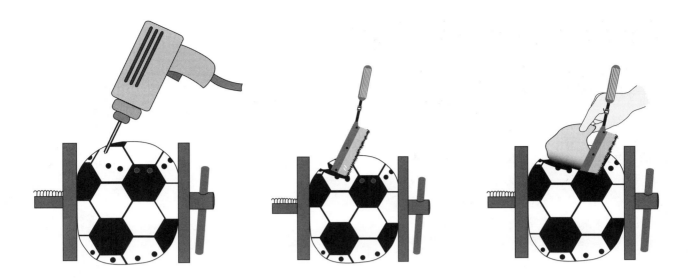

Drill 4 or 5 drainage holes in the ball.

Turn the ball over and secure it in the vise again. Drill a circle of holes in the top of the soccer ball to mark how large you'd like the opening to be. (Avoid the seams; it's difficult to drill through them.)

Use the saw or knife blade to carefully enlarge one of the holes. Slip the blade in and carefully cut from hole to hole.

2. Drill or poke some drainage holes in the sides of the cleats.

3. Fill the soccer ball and the cleats with the planting mix. Plant* your seeds or plants. Water* well.

4. Arrange your planters in a special place in the yard or on the patio. Water and fertilize regularly, and remove the dead flowers (see Off with Their Heads!, page 9).

Dive into Water Gardening

Water plants only look exotic — they're easy to grow. Colorful blossoms, intriguing leaves, "bubbling" grasses, and cool, refreshing water — all in a container! And almost any container will do, as long as it's waterproof. A plastic tub, a ceramic pot, a plastic wading pool (the rigid kind), even a metal container like an old washtub is fine as long as it's galvanized (coated so it won't rust).

What you need

4-gallon (16 L) or larger container
Topsoil*
Water plants (see AN UNDERWATER WORLD, page 28)
Clean water
Bricks (optional; see page 27)
Mosquito fish and aquatic snails (optional; see page 28)

See Quick Starts™ Growing Guide, pages 56–60.

Planting depth

Most bog plants are happiest in 1" to 4" (2.5 to 10 cm) of water (measure from the soil surface to the water level).

Oxygenating grasses should be submerged in no more than 24" (60 cm) of water.

What you do

If you're using a small or midsized container, you can plant the plants right in it. Fill the container half full of topsoil. Plant the plants in the soil (see page 58 for hole size and depth) and then slowly add clean water.

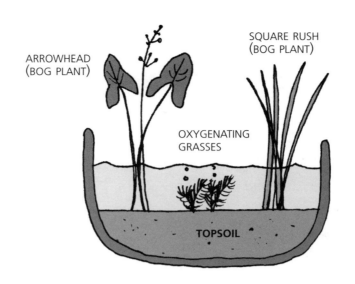

If you're using a larger container (like an old washtub), you can set potted plants (use 6"/15 cm-diameter pots filled with 3"/7.5 cm topsoil) right in it. This makes it easier to set a variety of plants at the right levels (plus, you won't need as much soil). Arrange the pots as shown, then slowly fill the tub. Add fish and snails, if using.

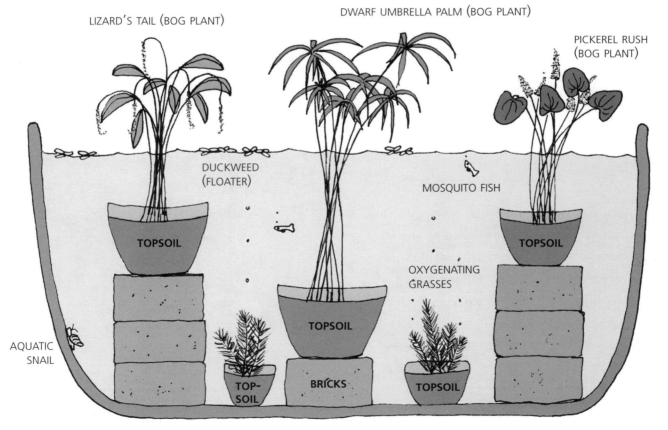

An underwater world

Your water garden is a self-contained mini-ecosystem (a community of plants and animals). A mix of different types of plants keeps everything healthy and in balance. If you have trouble finding water plants locally, see RESOURCES, *page 61.*

Bog plants *love to have wet feet! Some bloom; others just have cool-looking leaves. Here are some fun ones to try: arrowhead, dwarf umbrella palm (looks like a miniature palm tree!), lizard's tail, pennywort, pickerel rush, square rush (yes, the stems are four-sided!), water hyacinth*

WATER HYACINTH

Mosquito fish *and scavengers, like* **aquatic snails**, *will really bring your garden to life! They stay busy, too. The snails gobble up algae, keeping everything nice and clean, and the mosquito fish will make sure your water garden doesn't turn into "mosquito land" by gobbling up any eggs that are laid on the water.*

Floating plants *are real water-lovers — they don't need any soil! You just set them on top of the water, where they happily spread. Try Azollo, duckweed, and water clover.*

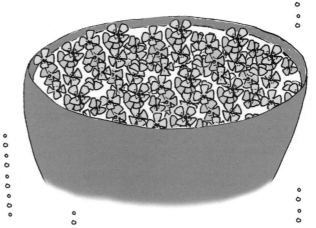

Oxygenating grasses *(Wow! That's a mouthful!) grow completely underwater, releasing oxygen. Look closely — can you see tiny bubbles rising? What's more, these grasses absorb the carbon dioxide gas given off by the decaying matter in your garden, which keeps excess algae from forming on the water. Some to look for include* Myriophyllum *and* Anacharis.

Pick-from-the-Lawn-Chair Strawberry Patch!

No weeding or other chores for this crop when you grow it in a container — just a load of ripe berries all within arm's reach for you to pluck and enjoy. You can use just about any large wooden, plastic, or ceramic container, or try a special planter called a strawberry jar (it has holes so plants can grow on the sides as well as at the top).

Your local garden center can recommend the best strawberry variety for your area and tell you how many plants you'll need for the size container you're going to use.

What you need

Strawberry plants
Container filled with planting
    mix*
Trowel
Hose or watering can
Fertilizer*

See Quick Starts™ Growing Guide, pages 56–60.

What you do

1. The most important thing when you plant strawberries is to get them at just the right depth. Set the plants in the planting mix as shown on page 30, spacing them about 6" (15 cm) apart.

   If you are using a strawberry jar, plant one plant in each hole in the side of the container as you fill it with the planting mix; then, plant the ones at the top.

Too shallow

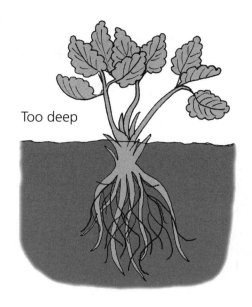

Too deep

2. Place the container in full sun. Keep the soil moist. (See WE'RE THIRSTY!, page 39)

3. Watch for the berries to ripen so that you can get to them before the birds do! *Mmmm ...* now that's the ultimate in summer flavor! Fertilize the plants once a week while they're producing berries.

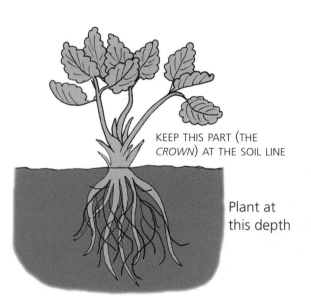

KEEP THIS PART (THE *CROWN*) AT THE SOIL LINE

Plant at this depth

SPREAD THE ROOTS OUT IN A FAN

Very Berry Sauce

Mash a pint (500 ml) of sliced fresh strawberries and sweeten to taste with 1 to 2 tablespoons (15 to 30 ml) of sugar. Serve over ice cream, yogurt, or pancakes for a super fresh-from-the-garden treat!

Digging Deeper:
Gardening in Small Spots & Backyard Plots

A pizza, a birdhouse, a flag of flowers, even a broom! Did you know you can grow all those things? Here you'll find fun things to grow and eat, lots of creative ideas for flower gardens, even ways to astonish your friends (how about the biggest pumpkin your neighborhood has ever seen, for starters?). So if you have an outdoor spot for these gardening adventures, grab your hoe and get ready to grow!

Incredible Edibles

Slice Up a Pizza Garden!

Planting a pizza garden is like ordering pizza toppings — go for just what you like! Your pizza garden can be small, medium, or large, as space permits (these instructions will make a 6'/2 m pizza-shaped garden).

What you need

Hammer or mallet
Stake
6' (2 m) circular sunny patch of
    soil* prepared for planting
4' (1.2 m) length of rope or string
Flour
Plants: basil, green peppers, onions (see GET SET
    FOR ONIONS!, page 33), oregano, parsley,
    tomatoes (see PASTE TOMATOES, page 33), or
    your own favorite pizza toppings (like
    summer squash or broccoli), annual* flowers
    (optional; see page 8)
Trowel
Hose or watering can
Fertilizer*

What you do

1. Pound the stake into the center of the planting area. Tie one end of the rope to the stake. Holding the other end of the rope, walk in a circle, sprinkling flour as you go, to form the outer edge of the "pie."

See Quick Starts™ Growing Guide, pages 56–60.

2. Use the rope and the flour to divide the pie in half and then to form an X. Now you have six "slices."

3. Plant* each section of the pizza pie. Fill in your herb slices with some colorful flowers, if you like. Keep your pizza garden watered*, fertilized, and weeded until it's time to harvest! Then, cook up your garden-fresh pickings in your favorite sauce recipe.

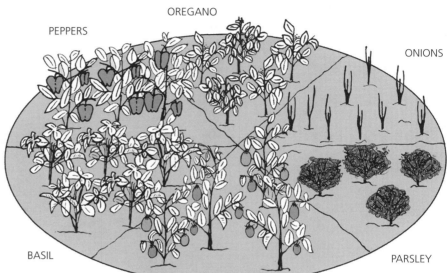

PEPPERS

OREGANO

ONIONS

BASIL

TOMATOES

PARSLEY

Paste tomatoes

Unlike the juicy tomatoes you slice into your salad, oval-shaped paste tomatoes have a meaty flesh that's perfect for making a thick, rich sauce. Check at your local garden center for varieties that will grow well in your area.

Get set for onions!

The easiest way to plant onions is to buy *sets*, tiny onions that have been grown for planting rather than for eating. You'll find them at the garden center and sometimes at the hardware store. Place the end with the dried roots in the garden, leaving the top half of the onion sticking out of the soil.

Grow Your Own Popcorn!

The next time you gather with a group of friends to watch your favorite videos, serve up your homegrown popcorn! You can even grow colorful kernels along with the traditional yellow ones.

What you need

8' x 8' (2.5 x 2.5 m) sunny
   patch of soil* prepared for
   planting
Seeds: popcorn
Hoe
Rake (optional)
Hose or watering can
Fertilizer*
Old screen (optional)
Old newspapers
Airtight jar

See Quick Starts™ Growing Guide, pages 56–60.

Do you have sweet corn, too?

If you'll also be growing sweet corn in your garden, you'll need to make some special arrangements to grow popcorn. (If the pollen from these two types of corn mixes, it will make your delicious sweet corn taste starchy.) Here are two things you can do:

- Separate the popcorn and the sweet corn plantings by at least 100' (30 m) and plant a row of tall sunflowers between them as a barrier.
- If you have a long enough growing season, choose a variety of sweet corn that will mature about a month before the popcorn is shedding its pollen.

What you do

To grow your popcorn

Corn *pollen* (the tiny, powdery grains that spread from plant to plant, fertilizing them) is carried by the wind, so when you plant in clumps rather than a few long rows, the pollen has a much better chance of spreading from plant to plant. And that means your ears of corn will be full of nice, fat kernels!

1. Plant* your seeds in a block of short rows (at least four) 2' (60 cm) apart. Or, plant corn Native American–style by raking the soil into small mounds and planting six seeds about 2" (5 cm) apart. Space the mounds about 2' (60 cm) apart.

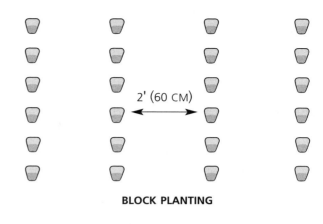

BLOCK PLANTING

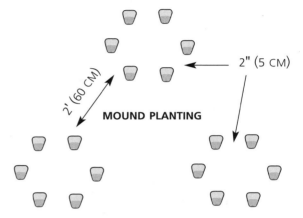

2' (60 CM)

2" (5 CM)

MOUND PLANTING

Quick Starts Tip!™

Fatten up those kernels

You can help your ears of corn grow big and fat! When you see the corn *tassel* (part of the male flower) at the top of the plant droop down, look for a yellow powder on the corn leaves below. Those are *pollen* grains (*a lot* of pollen grains, actually, since each one is only ½₅₀ of an inch/1 micrometer in diameter!); they need to get to the *silks* (those long strands at the top of the female flower lower down).

All you need to do is to give the stalk a good shake to send a few million pollen grains on their way. Way to go!

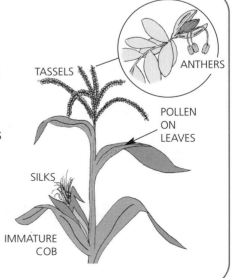

TASSELS

ANTHERS

POLLEN ON LEAVES

SILKS

IMMATURE COB

2. Keep the soil moist until the seedlings appear. Then water* and fertilize as needed.

To harvest and dry your popcorn

1. Leave the ears on the stalks until the husks are very dry and the kernels are hard. Harvest them (just pull down the ear and snap it off) before frost.

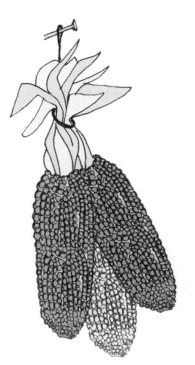

2. Pull back the husks and let the ears dry for about a month in a dry, airy location where they're safe from squirrels and birds (a screened porch or an attic is perfect). You can hang them by the husks or in a mesh bag, or you can spread them out on an old screen.

To shell and store your popcorn

Working over a sheet of old newspaper, push off the kernels with one hand while you twist the cob in the opposite direction with the other hand — it takes a little effort to get them off. Store the kernels in an airtight jar.

Over-the-Rainbow Veggie Garden

Does a purple pepper or a bright red ear of sweet corn taste better? Plant an edible rainbow and find out! This garden can be as big or as small as you like (a rough sketch of what's going where before you start to plant is always a good idea). You can also grow many of these vegetables in containers (see NO OUTDOOR SPOT FOR A GARDEN?, page 39, for tips).

What you need

Sunny patch of soil* prepared for planting
Plants or seeds: colorful varieties of vegetables
　　(see AN EDIBLE RAINBOW, page 38)
Hoe
Trowel
Hose or watering can
Fertilizer*

What you do

1. Plant* a selection of seeds and plants. Water* thoroughly and keep the soil moist until the seedlings appear.

2. Continue to weed and water throughout the season. Once your seeds are up, you'll need to do some thinning*. Fertilize and water regularly.

3. Harvest your vegetables as soon as they are large enough and brighten your table with bursting-with-color meals!

See Quick Starts™ Growing Guide, pages 56–60.

An edible rainbow

Did you know your favorite veggies came in these wild and wonderful colors? See RESOURCES, *page 61, if you can't find these varieties at the garden center.*

Purple Ruffles basil *(purple leaves)*

Chioggia beets *(red and white stripes inside)*

lemon cucumbers *(round, bright yellow cukes with a mild flavor)*

Red Sails lettuces *(green and deep red leaves)*

orange, purple, red, and yellow peppers: *Check your local garden center for the best varieties for your area.*

Lumina pumpkins *(white)*

Easter Egg radishes *(a mix of red, purple, and white radishes)*

Royal Burgundy string beans *(purple pods)*

Ruby Queen sweet corn: *red tassels, stalks, and cobs! (For tips on growing corn, see page 35.)*

Bright Lights Swiss chard: *leafy green tops on pink, orange, purple, red, and white stalks. It's awesome!*

yellow tomatoes: *Check your local garden center for the best varieties for your area.*

No outdoor spot for a garden?

This entire rainbow garden (except for the corn) will grow quite happily in containers. You probably already have items at home that you can use; a Styrofoam ice chest, a plastic bucket, a large plastic waste basket, an old bushel basket (lined with a plastic bag), even an old rigid plastic wading pool all make great garden planters — just poke some drainage holes in the bottom (and of course you'll check with a grown-up before you start filling them with dirt, right?).

Arrange the containers in their permanent spots; most vegetables and flowers need lots of sunshine, but leafy crops like lettuce and chard and root crops like beets will do fine with some shade. Fill the containers about three-fourths full of the planting mix*. Plant* your seeds or plants and water (see below).

See FAST-FOOD WINDOWSILL SALAD GARDEN (pages 5 to 7), SOCCER STAR'S GARDEN (pages 24 to 25), and SOW A SUNFLOWER PARADE (pages 44 to 45) for more outdoor container-gardening ideas.

Quick Starts Tips!™

We're thirsty!

The key to happy container plants is enough water. Check them *daily* — containers, especially small ones, dry out quickly, particularly when the weather is hot, dry, or windy. Poke your finger about halfway into the soil — if it feels dry, it's time to water. Wet the soil until water starts to come out of the bottom of the container, then stop. If you use saucers under the planters, don't leave the plants sitting in water.

See Quick Starts™ Growing Guide, pages 56–60.

Flower Power

Open a Butterfly Café

Want to bring your yard alive with colorful butterflies? Put their favorite kinds of nectar on the menu and they won't be able to resist! Butterflies will really appreciate the energy boost in the mid- to late summer, when they're most active.

or

What you need

Sunny patch of soil* prepared for planting or a large planter filled with planting mix*

Plants or seeds (see BUTTERFLY FAVES!, page 41)

Trowel or hoe

Hose or watering can

Fertilizer*

What you do

1. Plant* your plants or seeds in the garden. If you're planting in a container, choose flowers from the annuals* list (page 41) — and be sure to put your planter near a comfortable lawn chair so you can sit and watch the butterflies.

> ### Butterflies are in search of ...
>
> a **sunny spot** out of the wind where they can warm their wings. Locate your butterfly planting in a protected spot and set a large flat rock near it for a warm resting spot.
>
> **nectar**, a sweet substance in the flowers that gives butterflies lots of energy for all that fluttering.
>
> a nice, cool drink of **water**! Be sure to provide a "butterfly puddle" (a shallow container set in or near the garden and filled with water) so they can stop and sip.

See Quick Starts™ Growing Guide, pages 56–60.

2. Keep your garden watered* and weeded. Snip off the dead flower blossoms (see OFF WITH THEIR HEADS!, page 9) and fertilize regularly, so that the plants will keep blooming throughout the summer.

Is it a butterfly or a moth?

If you see it during the day, chances are it's a butterfly. Moths are more active at night. Watch it land: If it holds its wings up, it's a butterfly. If it rests with its wings down, it's a moth.

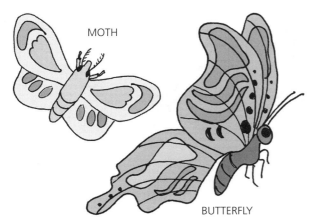

MOTH

BUTTERFLY

Butterfly faves!

Butterflies are attracted to red, orange, yellow, purple, and pink. Plant in clumps of a single color so they can easily zero in on the flowers.

Annuals*

cosmos
marigolds
nicotiana (comes
    in a range of
    colors; choose
    red or pink)
petunias (comes in
    a range of col-
    ors; choose red,
    pink, or purple)
zinnias

Perennials*

asters
bee balm
black-eyed Susans
butterfly bush (a
    shrub)
butterfly weed
daisies
daylilies
goldenrod
milkweed
purple coneflower
yarrow

Plant a Bright-Blooming flag

Feeling patriotic? How about a bright-colored flag of flowers to flutter and wave in the breeze! Bright-colored, easy-to-grow petunias are the perfect choice for your living flag.

What you need

Stakes
String
Sunny plot of soil* prepared for
    planting
Flour
Plants: red, white, and blue
    petunias
Trowel
Hose or watering can
Fertilizer*

See Quick Starts™ Growing Guide, pages 56–60.

What you do

1. Use stakes and string to mark the edges of the flag.

2. Use the flour to mark the sections of the flag. You don't need to show all 50 stars — a few rows will be enough to give the idea.

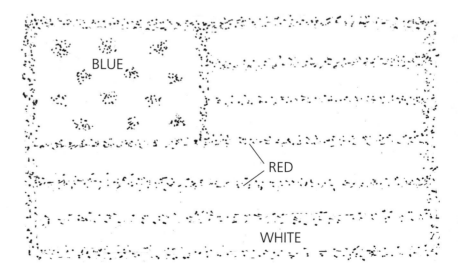

BLUE

RED

WHITE

3. Plant* the petunias. Water* them well.

4. To keep your flag in full bloom, visit it every day to pull off the old flower blossoms (see OFF WITH THEIR HEADS!, page 9). Fertilize regularly.

High-Flying Flags

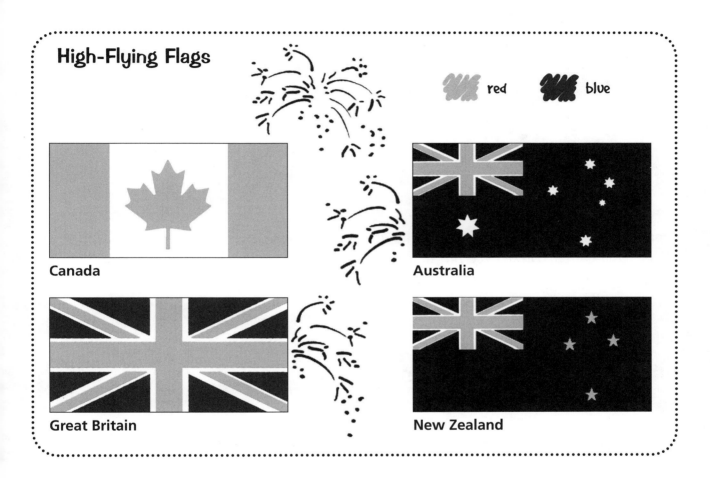

red   blue

Canada

Australia

Great Britain

New Zealand

✿ More Garden Fun!

Sign your name with flowers. *Spell out the letters of your name with brightly colored flowers. "Write" your name with flour on the soil to form the letters. Then plant one color of flower for each letter.*

Sow a Sunflower Parade

From just-reach-your-knees small to scrape-the-sky tall, here's a sunflower collection in all shapes and colors! These cheerful flowers can march right along the edge of the garden, or fill a small spot in the yard. (No room for a parade? Several of the smaller sunflower varieties grow quite happily in containers.) They'll give you loads of big, bright bouquets all season long — and then turn into homegrown bird feeders!

What you need

Sunny rectangular plot of soil* prepared for planting or a large planter filled with planting mix*

Seeds: sunflowers (see SUNFLOWERS FROM SMALL TO TALL, page 45)

Trowel or hoe

Hose or watering can

*See Quick Starts™ Growing Guide, pages 56–60.

What you do

1. Plant* the seeds in a row from the smallest variety to the tallest. Keep the soil moist until the seedlings emerge.

2. Watch them grow! Sunflowers are just about the easiest flowers you can raise. All they really ask for is a spot that's stays sunny all day and if the soil gets really dry, they'll appreciate a drink of water*, especially while they're still small. You don't even need to worry about weeding, unless things really get out of hand, because they're such big, sturdy plants.

Sunflowers from small to tall

Garden centers and seed catalogs offer an amazing selection of sunflowers in all shapes, sizes and colors. Here are some suggestions for a striking parade, from 12" to 15' (30 cm to 4 m) tall, with colors from dark red to orange to pale yellow! The catalogs listed in RESOURCES, page 62, carry these sunflowers and many others. Those 2' (60 cm) and under are perfect for containers.

1' to 2' (30 to 60 cm)	Pacino (yellow), Sundance Kid (bronze to yellow, some two-color) — good choice for containers
2' to 2½' (60 to 75 cm)	Music Box (yellow, orange, deep red) — also great for containers
3' to 4' (1 m)	Floristan (dark red with light yellow tips), Sonja (light orange)
4' to 5' (1.5 m)	Ikarus (bright yellow)
5' to 6' (1.75 m)	Soraya (orange), Sunbright (orange), Valentine (pale yellow)
6' to 7' (2 m)	Moulin Rouge (deep red), Giant Sungold (big pom-pom–like orange blossoms — if you only try one from this list, go for this one!)
9' to 12' (3 m)	Mammoth Russian (also called California Greystripe). The old-fashioned tall type with a single yellow bright blossom at the top; birds love this one!
12' to 15' (4 m)	Paul Bunyan Hybrid (yellow), Kong (yellow). Now *that's* tall! More bird favorites, too!

Quick Starts Tips!™

Bring on the birds

Don't cut *all* your sunflower blossoms for bouquets. If you leave some flowers on the plants, they'll produce big heads full of seeds, and sunflower seeds are the birds' all-time favorite food! They gobble them right off the plants. Or, you can cut the flower heads and place them on the deck, patio, or other place where you can watch the birds feast up close.

Fun in the Sun

A Gourd-geous Birdhouse

*Did you know you can grow a birdhouse? A dried gourd
makes a cozy home for many different kinds of birds and it
will last for years. Gourds come in lots of shapes and sizes,
but it's easy to remember which ones are best for birdhouses
because they're called — you guessed it! — birdhouse gourds.
They're also called* bottle *or* dipper *gourds. (See* RESOURCES,
page 61, if you can't find them at the garden center.)

What you need

Sunny patch of soil* prepared
    for planting or large
    container filled with
    planting mix*

Seeds: any bottle-shaped gourd

Trowel

Wire fencing and string or
    strips of cloth (optional)

Hose or watering can

Sharp knife (for use with
    grown-up help)

Vinegar

Water

Mesh bags

Quick Starts Tips!™

Gourds like it hot!

You'll need at least four months between the
frost dates* for your area to grow gourds to
maturity. If your gardening season is short, plan
on starting the seeds indoors* (see GROW A
PUMPED-UP PUMPKIN!, step 1, page 51) and then
planting* them outdoors when the weather
warms up.

See Quick Starts™ Growing Guide, pages 56–60.

What you do

To grow your gourds

1. Plant* the seeds. (For container-gardening tips, see No Outdoor Spot for a Garden?, page 39.)

2. If you keep the vines off the ground, the plants will take up less space and the gourds will have nicely rounded shapes. As the vines grow, tie them loosely to a section of wire fencing or train them along a fence or the lower branches of a nearby tree. Keep the plants watered* and weeded.

To harvest and dry your gourds

1. Watch for the leaves to die and the stems to turn brown. With some varieties, the color of the gourd will also change. Cut each gourd with at least 1" (2.5 cm) of stem and keep only gourds with smooth, unblemished skins.

2. Wash the gourds in a mild vinegar solution (1 cup/250 ml vinegar to 3 quarts/2 L water). This will take care of any mold or bacteria on the outside of the gourds that might cause them to rot.

3. Place each gourd in a mesh bag (an old onion bag is perfect) and hang in a warm, dry, airy place out of direct sunlight. Let the gourds dry for at least a month; some varieties will take several months. Shake the gourd — if the seeds rattle, the gourd is ready.

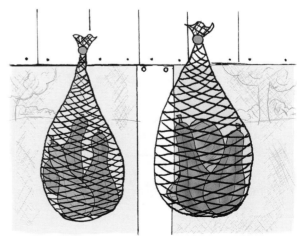

To make your birdhouse

What you need

Dried gourd

Drill, ¼" (5 mm) drill bit, a drill bit or speed bore
for the size entrance hole you want (see
COME ON IN!, page 49) or a small keyhole saw

Bench vise

Ruler or tape measure

Wire coat hanger

Varnish or paint

Paintbrush

Note: Please ask a grown-up for help in using
all of these tools.

Meet the cucurbits!

*What is a gourd, exactly? It's a
cucurbit (kew-CUR-bit), a big family
of rambling vines that includes winter
squashes like buttercup and butternut,
as well as zucchini, yellow squash,
pumpkins, and even cucumbers and
melons.*

*See Quick Starts™ Growing Guide, pages 56–60.

What you do

1. The skin of a dried gourd is *hard*, so
   you'll need a grown-up to help you make
   these holes. Secure the gourd in the vise.
   Drill a hole through the top of the gourd.

Drill several ¼" (5 mm) drainage holes in
the bottom. Drill or saw a round entrance
hole in the gourd (see COME ON IN!, page
49, for recommended sizes) and shake out
the dried seeds.

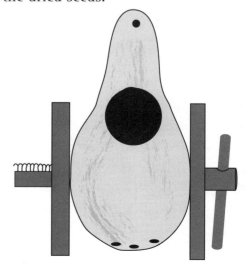

2. Push the hook of the coat hanger through the top hole. Straighten the hanger.

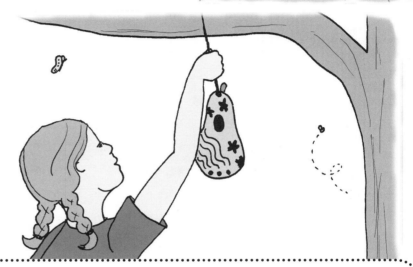

STRAIGHTENED HANGER

3. Again with a grown-up's help, apply several coats of varnish to seal the outside (it's smelly stuff — be sure to work outdoors or where there is good ventilation). If you want to use the house for purple martins, paint it white. Brown or green is a good choice for other birds.

4. Hang the birdhouse from a tree branch or a horizontal wire with the opening away from the wind, if possible.

Come on In!

The size of the entrance hole will determine the type of bird that will use your birdhouse. Make the hole in the upper third of the gourd; many birds like to settle down in the bottom of their house, plus it keeps the babies from falling out.

Look for one or more of these birds to visit your gourdhouses; they're found throughout most of the continental United States and the southern half of Canada.

Type of bird	Length of gourd	Entrance hole
Chickadee	6" (15 cm)	1½" (3.5 cm)
Downy woodpecker	8" (20 cm)	1¼" (3 cm)
Hairy woodpecker	12" (30 cm)	1⅝" (4 cm)
House wren	6" (15 cm)	1" (2.5 cm)
Nuthatch	8" (20 cm)	1¼" (3 cm)
Purple martin	10" (25 cm)	2½" (6 cm)

Grow a Pumped-up Pumpkin!

With a little special care, you can have a vine-bustin' blockbuster of a pumpkin to amaze your friends and neighbors (and maybe win a prize)! But you will need a fair amount of garden space — a pumpkin vine can ramble for a good 15' to 20' (4.5 to 6 m).

What you need

Seeds: large pumpkin variety such as Big Max, Dill's Atlantic Giant, or Prizewinner (check your local garden center or see RESOURCES, page 61)

Peat pots*

Planting mix*

Bag of composted manure*

Large, sunny circular area of soil* prepared for planting

Rake

Trowel

Hose or watering can

Plastic milk jug or bucket (optional)

Fertilizer*

Tape measure

Sharp knife (for use with grown-up help)

See Quick Starts™ Growing Guide, pages 56–60.

Keeping track in the pumpkin patch

A garden journal (see MY GREEN-THUMB JOURNAL, pages 10 to 11) will come in handy when you're trying to "super size" it.

- **Note when you start** your seeds and when you transplant so you'll know when to start looking for those first blossoms to pollinate (see WHAT YOU DO, step 5, page 52).
- **Measure the little pumpkins** and record their growth to help you decide which one is the keeper (step 6) — this may be your most important decision.
- **Once you've selected your champ**, measure it weekly. Make sure it's getting enough water* (see MAKE A RAIN GAUGE, page 16) and keep track of when you fertilize.

What you do

1. Even if you usually plant pumpkin seeds right in the garden, it's best to give your jumbo pumpkins a head start indoors. About four weeks before the last spring frost date*, plant one seed (pointed end facing down) in each peat pot. Place the peat pots in a warm, sunny spot and don't let the planting mix dry out.

2. Once the plants have their first set of true leaves* (or the roots are starting to poke out of the bottom of the peat pots), it's time to plant* them in the garden. Sprinkle the manure over the circular area and rake the soil into a large mound (about 18"/45 cm in diameter).

3. Dig two holes slightly larger than the peat pots. Pick your two healthiest-looking plants and set the peat pots right into the mound so that you won't disturb the roots of the baby plants. Water* them well.

If necessary, use a plastic milk jug with the bottom cut off or even a plastic bucket to protect the little plants from frost or wind.

4. Pumpkins, especially these jumbo kinds, are hungry plants! Fertilize them once a week during the growing season.

5. Now, here's the real key to having the biggest pumpkin on the block: You'll have to play the part of a bee and hand-pollinate the flowers. Pollinating the flowers means you'll get a pumpkin to *set*, or start to grow, as early as possible. And you want your monster pumpkin to have all the growing days it can get! The more blossoms you pollinate, the better your chances of getting an early grower. It's not hard, but you'll have to be an early riser, because you have to use freshly opened blossoms that haven't wilted in the heat of the day.

First, look for the female flowers. They're the ones with the tiny little green pumpkins at their bases, and they appear about 8 to 10 weeks after you started your seeds.

Now, pick a male flower (that's right, no tiny pumpkin) that just opened. Pull off the outer petals to expose the *pollen* (the yellow powdery stuff that fertilizes the plant). Gently brush the center of the female flower with the male flower. *Buzz, buzz!*

6. Once your potential prizewinners are off and growing, keep checking the stem.

The stem should look like this.

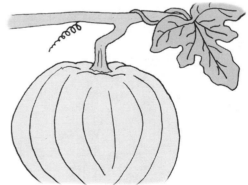

This stem might snap.

Adjust yours slowly and gently over several days so that you don't disturb the pumpkin or hurt the stem. You may need to support either the pumpkin or the vine with boards to get the proper angle.

7. OK, now here's the hard part: After your pumpkins have been growing for a couple of weeks, you'll have to choose the best one per plant and remove the others. That's right, you've got to cut off those other healthy pumpkins! Why? Well, you do want all the plant's energy to go into pumping up just one monster pumpkin, don't you?

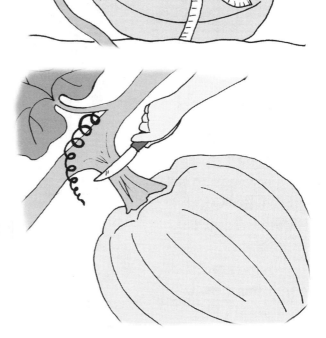

Measure the pumpkins around their middles. Choose the largest one that's growing the fastest. Here's where your journal will come in handy (see KEEPING TRACK IN THE PUMPKIN PATCH, page 50). Examine their shapes, too. Tall pumpkins tend to be the largest. Then, cut off all the other pumpkins (see step 8), being careful not to damage the main vine.

8. About 10' or 12' (3 to 3.5 m) beyond the remaining pumpkin, cut the vine. Keep the side shoots trimmed back, too.

9. Let your pumpkin pile on the pounds right up until frost is predicted for your area, then harvest it. Cut the stem, leaving about 2" to 3" (5 to 7.5 cm).

More Garden fun!

Personalize your pumpkin. *Carve your name or a secret message on the side of your pumpkin when it's small — the words will grow right along with the pumpkin!*

You Can Grow a Broom!

Maybe even a Nimbus 2000! But even if you don't take to the Quidditch field, you'll still have to clean your room, so make it more fun with a home-grown broom.

What you need

Sunny patch of soil* prepared for planting

Seeds: broomcorn, also called sorghum (see CAN'T FIND BROOMCORN?, page 55)

Hoe

Hose or watering can

Sharp knife (for use with grown-up help)

Old sheet or blanket

Twine or string

Wooden dowel or long, straight branch (optional)

*See Quick Starts™ Growing Guide, pages 56–60.

What you do

To grow your broomcorn

In mid- to late spring, plant* your seeds. Once the plants are up and growing, stand back! They can get to be anywhere from 5' to 10' (1.5 to 3 m) tall! Keep them watered* and weeded. About 105 to 110 days after seeding, your corn should be ready. The stalks will have tall tufts of greenish gold, bronze, or black seedheads.

To dry and thresh the stalks

1. Cut the plants at the bottom and hang them upside down for several weeks in a dry, airy place until they are completely dry.

2. Now, here's the fun part! To remove all the seeds, called *threshing*, spread an old sheet or blanket on the ground and whack the stalks against it. (Save the seeds for the birds — they love them!)

To make a broom

If the stems of your plants are sturdy enough, just wind twine tightly around a bunch of them. If not, put a wooden dowel or a long, straight branch in the middle of the bunch of stalks to stiffen it before wrapping the twine.

Quick Starts Tips!™

Can't find broomcorn?

Broomcorn isn't really corn, it's *sorghum*. The stalk looks like corn when the plant is growing, but it doesn't develop any ears. Like corn (and oats and wheat), sorghum is a grain. It originally came from Africa, where it's one of the most important food crops. If you can't find seeds at the local garden center (remember to look for both names), see RESOURCES, page 62.

Now you're ready to chase that Golden Snitch!

Quick Starts™ Growing Guide

Annuals

These flower or vegetable plants grow in your garden for one season and then die. You need to replant them each season.

Fertilizer (see also Manure)

You might already know that plants make their own food using the sun's energy (a process called *photosynthesis*). But to do that, they take nutrients out of the soil. So that your plants keep growing and producing fruit or flowers all through the gardening season, it's a good idea to *replenish* (put back) those soil nutrients.

For flowers, fruits, and veggies, water-soluble fertilizers like liquid seaweed are really easy to use — a measured amount goes right into the watering can so you can take care of two jobs at once. Just follow the instructions on the label. For indoor plants, look for a houseplant fertilizer.

Frost dates

Gardeners often talk about "the last spring frost date" and "the first fall frost date" for the areas where they live. The last spring frost date refers to the latest date in spring when frost typically occurs. After that date, you usually figure you're safe to plant crops that would be killed by frost. The first fall frost date is at the other end of the gardening season. It's the date in the fall when the first frost usually occurs, killing plants that are sensitive to cold temperatures. To find out those dates for your area, check with the Extension Service of your state university, the local office of the National Weather Service (U.S.) or the Meteorological Service of Canada, or a local garden center.

Manure (see also Fertilizer)

Manure is an inexpensive fertilizer that's easy to work into the soil at planting time. If you want all the gory details, it's animal waste, typically from a cow. (And before you say *Eew!*, wait until you see what it does for your plants!) *Composted*, or *dried* manure, has been processed so that it doesn't include a lot of weed seeds and won't burn the roots of plants. (And one other thing is missing — the smell!) Composted cow manure is readily available in bags at garden centers — look for names like Moo Doo.

Peat pots

These little pots made of compressed peat moss are great for starting seeds indoors because the plants can later go right into the garden, pot and all!

Perennials

These plants live from year to year (even in a cold climate, where they may die back completely in winter, they'll start growing again in the spring). In most climates, perennial flowers don't bloom their first year of growth, so rather than grow them from seed, many gardeners buy perennials as plants at the garden center.

Planting

Planting seeds outdoors

All the information you need to plant your seeds is right on the seed packet. It will tell you, for example, when to plant those seeds outdoors in your *zone* (climate region).

Once you've prepared the soil (see page 59), use a hoe or trowel to make a furrow in the soil (mark the row with stakes and string, if you like).

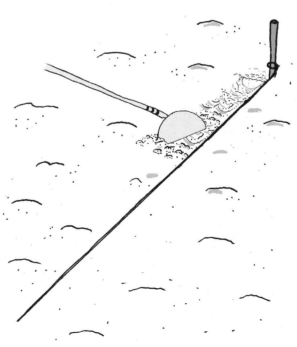

Sprinkle the seeds in the furrow. The seed packet will tell you how deep and how far apart to place seeds. Cover them with soil and pat it down. Keep the seed packet so you'll remember what you planted and know when to transplant (see below) if you are starting seeds indoors.

Planting plants

When you buy plants at a garden center or start them from seeds indoors, you'll need to plant them outdoors (called *transplanting*). Transplanting can be a shock to young plants, so expose them gradually to outdoor temperatures and bright sunlight before you plant them outdoors. Late afternoon or cloudy days are the best times for transplanting; this gives the seedlings time to settle in a bit before it gets really hot and sunny.

Prepare the soil (see page 59). Dig a hole as deep as and slightly wider than your plant.

Set the seedling into the hole, keeping as much of the soil around the roots as possible. Fill in the hole and firm the soil around the plant. Water well (see page 60).

Here's how to remove the plant from the pot:

Gently work the plant loose, holding it by the leaves, never by the stem.

Planting mix

You can purchase various types of planting mixes in bags at the hardware store or garden center. A *soilless mix* is a combination of natural materials like peat moss, *vermiculite* (tiny, lightweight volcanic rocks), and sometimes fertilizer to make a fluffy, soil-like substance that drains well and is free of the diseases and weed seeds that might be lurking in garden soil. It's perfect for container gardening because it's so lightweight. You can use it for starting seeds indoors, too. Premoistening the mix makes it easier to work with. *Potting soil* is a good choice for houseplants and container gardening.

Soil, preparing for planting

Taking the time to prepare the soil will mean a more successful garden. Yank out any weeds, even the little ones. Then, loosen the top 6" (15 cm) of soil with a pitchfork. Don't go much deeper or you'll wake up a lot of weed seeds sleeping down below! You just want to loosen the top clumps of soil and make the top layer nice and fluffy.

Then, rake the area with a back and forth motion (kind of like vacuuming) until you have a smooth, level area, ready for planting.

To reuse an outdoor container, pull out the old plants and break up the clumps of roots in the top layer of the planting mix. Add fresh mix (see page 58) and smooth it out.

Thinning

Usually you plant more seeds than you really need, in case some don't sprout. It can get a little crowded if most — or all! — of them pop up. Once the seedlings are up and growing, remove some so that each remaining one has enough room around it to grow and develop properly. Check the seed packet for spacing guidelines.

Topsoil

It's the dark rich upper layer of soil where most of the nutrients usually are. Look for it in bags at the garden center.

True leaves

The first leaves to appear when a seed *germinates* (sprouts) are the seed leaves, or *cotyledons*. These leaves are full of stored energy that gets the seed up and growing. They're followed by the first real leaves (called *true leaves*).

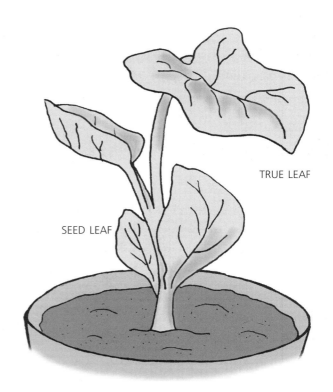

TRUE LEAF

SEED LEAF

Watering

When you water, evenly wet the soil to a depth of at least 6"/15 cm, rather than only sprinkling the top layer of soil. With deep watering, the plants develop deep roots, which helps them survive during dry weather. (For tips on watering container-grown plants, see page 39.)

Roots with shallow watering

Roots with deep watering

Resources

For the vegetables and flowers mentioned in this book, check a local garden center first. If it doesn't carry that specific variety, it may offer something similar; ask a salesperson. For the water gardening and carnivorous plants, try a local florist or greenhouse. For mail-order sources, see below. You'll find contact information for each seed company on page 62.

Bring on the Bug-Munchers!

pitcher plant, sundew, Venus flytrap: Exotic Gardens; Fly-Trap Farm

Dive into Water Gardening

water-gardening plants and supplies: Lilypons Water Gardens; Van Ness Water Gardens

Fast-Food Windowsill Salad Garden (Mini-Munches)

Easter Egg radish: W. Atlee Burpee & Co.; Johnny's Selected Seeds; Park Seed Company; Shepherd's Garden Seeds; Territorial Seed Company

Evergreen Long White Bunching scallion: W. Atlee Burpee & Co.; Nichols Garden Nursery; Park Seed Company

Little Ball beet: W. Atlee Burpee & Co.

Little Finger carrot: W. Atlee Burpee & Co.; Park Seed Company; Seeds of Change

Little Gem lettuce: Park Seed Company; Shepherd's Garden Seeds; Territorial Seed Company

Thumbelina carrot: W. Atlee Burpee & Co.; Nichols Garden Nursery; Park Seed Company; Territorial Seed Company

Tom Thumb lettuce: Nichols Garden Nursery; Seeds of Change; Shepherd's Garden Seeds; Southern Exposure Seed Exchange; Territorial Seed Company

Space spinach: Johnny's Selected Seeds; Park Seed Company

A Gourd-geous Birdhouse

birdhouse, bottle, or dipper gourds: W. Atlee Burpee & Co.; Johnny's Selected Seeds; Nichols Garden Nursery; Park Seed Company; Seeds of Change; Southern Exposure Seed Exchange; Territorial Seed Company

Grow a Pumped-Up Pumpkin!

Big Max: W. Atlee Burpee & Co.; Seeds of Change

Dill's Atlantic Giant: Howard Dill Enterprises; Johnny's Selected Seeds; Nichols Garden Nursery; Territorial Seed Company

Prizewinner: W. Atlee Burpee & Co.; Johnny's Selected Seeds; Nichols Garden Nursery; Territorial Seed Company

Grow Your Own Popcorn!

colored and yellow popcorn varieties: W. Atlee Burpee & Co.; Johnny's Selected Seeds; Nichols Garden Nursery; Southern Exposure Seed Exchange; Territorial Seed Company

Over-the-Rainbow Veggie Garden (An Edible Rainbow)

Bright Lights Swiss chard: W. Atlee Burpee & Co.; Johnny's Selected Seeds; Park Seed Company; Shepherd's Garden Seeds; Stokes Seeds; Territorial Seed Company

Chioggia beet: W. Atlee Burpee & Co.; Johnny's Selected Seeds; Nichols Garden Nursery; Seeds of Change; Shepherd's Garden Seeds; Southern Exposure Seed Exchange; Territorial Seed Company

Easter Egg radish: W. Atlee Burpee & Co.; Johnny's Selected Seeds; Park Seed Company; Shepherd's Garden Seeds; Territorial Seed Company

lemon cucumber: W. Atlee Burpee & Co.; Nichols Garden Nursery; Park Seed Company; Seeds of Change; Shepherd's Garden Seeds; Southern Exposure Seed Exchange; Territorial Seed Company

Lumina pumpkin: W. Atlee Burpee & Co.; Park Seed Company; Stokes Seeds; Territorial Seed Company

Purple Ruffles basil: W. Atlee Burpee & Co.; Johnny's Selected Seeds; Park Seed Company; Shepherd's Garden Seeds; Southern Exposure Seed Exchange; Territorial Seed Company

Red Sails lettuce: Johnny's Selected Seeds; Nichols Garden Nursery; Park Seed Company; Southern Exposure Seed Exchange; Stokes Seeds; Territorial Seed Company

Royal Burgundy string bean: Seeds of Change; Stokes Seeds; Territorial Seed Company

Ruby Queen sweet corn: W. Atlee Burpee & Co.

Sow a Sunflower Parade

Floristan: Johnny's Selected Seeds; Shepherd's Garden Seeds; Territorial Seed Company

Giant Sungold: Johnny's Selected Seeds; Park Seed Company, Territorial Seed Company

Ikarus: Johnny's Selected Seeds; Shepherd's Garden Seeds

Kong: Shepherd's Garden Seeds; Territorial Seed Company

Mammoth Russian (California Greystripe): W. Atlee Burpee & Co.; Johnny's Selected Seeds; Shepherd's Garden Seeds; Southern Exposure Seed Exchange; Stokes Seeds

Moulin Rouge: Johnny's Selected Seeds; Shepherd's Garden Seeds; Stokes Seeds

Music Box: Park Seed Company; Shepherd's Garden Seeds; Territorial Seed Company

Pacino: Johnny's Selected Seeds; Park Seed Company; Stokes Seeds; Territorial Seed Company

Paul Bunyan Hybrid: W. Atlee Burpee & Co.

Sonja: Johnny's Selected Seeds; Park Seed Company; Southern Exposure Seed Exchange; Stokes Seeds

Soraya: W. Atlee Burpee & Co.; Johnny's Selected Seeds; Park Seed Company; Stokes Seeds; Territorial Seed Company

Sunbright: W. Atlee Burpee & Co., Johnny's Selected Seeds; Territorial Seed Company

Sundance Kid: W. Atlee Burpee & Co.; Johnny's Selected Seeds; Park Seed Company; Shepherd's Garden Seeds

Valentine: Johnny's Selected Seeds; Park Seed Company; Shepherd's Garden Seeds; Territorial Seed Company

Welcome Your Worms!

red wigglers and vermicomposting supplies: Cape Cod Worm Farm; Happy D Ranch; National Gardening Association

You Can Grow a Broom!

sorghum (broomcorn): W. Atlee Burpee & Co.; Johnny's Selected Seeds; Seeds of Change, Territorial Seed Company

ADDRESSES

W. Atlee Burpee & Co., 300 Park Ave., Warminster, PA 18974; (800) 333-5808; <*www.burpee.com*>

Cape Cod Worm Farm, 30 Center Ave., Buzzards Bay, MA 02532; (508) 759-5664; <*members.aol.com/Capeworms/private/wormhome.htm*>

Exotic Gardens, P.O. Box 609, Cypress, TX 77410; (281) 374-6958; <*petflytrap.com*>

Fly-Trap Farm, 1929 Civietown Rd. SW, Supply, NC 28462; (866) 838-3276; <*www.flytrapfarm.com*>

Happy D Ranch, P.O. Box 3001, Visalia, CA 93278; (888) 989-1558; <*www.happydranch.com*>

Howard Dill Enterprises, RR 1, 400 College Rd., Windsor, Nova Scotia, Canada B0N 2T0; <*www.howarddill.com*>

Johnny's Selected Seeds, 184 Foss Hill Rd., Albion, ME 04910; (207) 437-4357; <*www.johnnyseeds.com*>

Lilypons Water Gardens, 6800 Lilypons Rd., Buckeystown, MD 21717-0010; (800) 999-5459; <*www.lilypons.com*>

National Gardening Association, 1100 Dorset St., South Burlington, VT 05403; (800) 538-7476; <*www.kidsgardening.org*>

Nichols Garden Nursery, 1190 Old Salem Rd. NE, Albany, OR, 97321-4580; (800) 422-3985; <*www.nicholsgardennursery.com*>

Park Seed Company, 1 Parkton Ave., Greenwood, SC 29649; (800) 213-0076; <*www.parkseed.com*>

Seeds of Change, P.O. Box 15700, Santa Fe, NM 87506; (888) 762-7333; <*www.seedsofchange.com*>

Shepherd's Garden Seeds, 30 Irene St., Torrington, CT 06790-6658; (860) 482-3638; <*www.shepherdseeds.com*>

Southern Exposure Seed Exchange, P.O. Box 460, Mineral, VA 23117; (540) 894-9480; <*www.southernexposure.com*>

Stokes Seeds, P.O. Box 548, Buffalo, NY 14240-0548; (716) 695-6980; <*www.stokeseeds.com*>

Territorial Seed Company, P.O. Box 158, Cottage Grove, OR 97424-0061; (541) 942-9547; <*www.territorial-seed.com*>

Van Ness Water Gardens, 2460 North Euclid Ave., Upland, CA 91784-1199; (800) 205-2425; <*www.vnwg.com*>

Index